Understanding the
Declaration of Independence

James Wolfe and Jennifer Viega

Enslow Publishing
101 W. 23rd Street
Suite 240
New York, NY 10011
USA

enslow.com

Published in 2016 by Enslow Publishing, LLC.
101 W. 23rd Street, Suite 240, New York, NY 10011

Library of Congress Cataloging-in-Publication Data
Wolfe, James, 1960-
  Understanding the Declaration of Independence / James Wolfe and Jennifer Viegas.
    pages cm. — (Primary sources of American political documents)
  Summary: "Discusses the creation and execution of the Declaration of Independence in the early days of the United States"—Provided by publisher.
  Includes bibliographical references and index.
  ISBN 978-0-7660-6874-2
  1. United States. Declaration of Independence—Juvenile literature. 2. United States—Politics and government—1775-1783—Juvenile literature. I. Viegas, Jennifer. II. Title.
  E221.W75 2016
  973.3'13—dc23
                        2015008039

Printed in the United States of America

To Our Readers: We have done our best to make sure all Web site addresses in this book were active and appropriate when we went to press. However, the author and the publisher have no control over and assume no liability for the material available on those Web sites or on any Web sites they may link to. Any comments or suggestions can be sent by e-mail to customerservice@enslow.com.

Photo Credits: Alexander Gardner/Hulton Archive/Getty Images, p. 88; Allies Interactive/Shutterstock.com (title page, front matter, back matter, and chapter openers); Augusto Cabral/Shutterstock.com (primary source corner dingbat); DEA Picture/De Agostini Picture Library/Getty Images, pp. 1, 21, 62, 70; Education Images/UIG/Getty Images, p. 79; Everett Historical/Shutterstock.com, p.12; Fine Art Images/Superstock/Getty Images, p. 29; Hisham Ibrahim/Photographer's Choice/Getty Images, p. 59; John Parrot/Stockstreck Images/Getty Images, p. 37; Library of Congress Prints and Photographs Division, pp. 24, 27, 31, 33, 43, 47, 56, 64; © Mary Evans Picture Library Ltd./age fotostock, p. 34; Photo Researchers/Science Source/Getty Images, p. 45; Photri Images/Superstock/Getty Images, p. 5; Superstock/Getty Images, pp. 17, 41, 68; Stanislav Pobytov/Vetta/Getty images, p. 10; traveler1116/E+/Getty Images, p. 53.

Cover Credits: DEA Picture/De Agostini Picture Library/Getty Images (Founding Fathers); Allies Interactive/Shutterstock.com (title splash); Augusto Cabral/Shutterstock.com (logo and spine button).

Contents

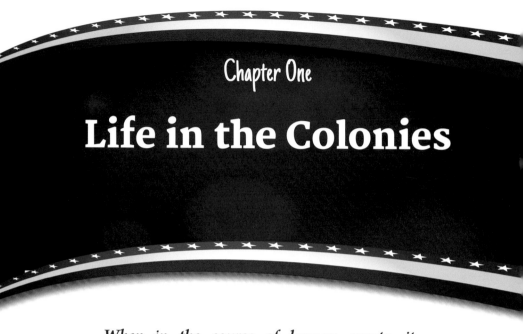

Chapter One

Life in the Colonies

When in the course of human events, it becomes necessary for one People to dissolve the Political Bands which have connected them with another, and to assume among the Powers of the Earth, the separate and equal Station to which the Laws of Nature and Nature's God entitle them, a decent Respect for the Opinions of Mankind requires that they should declare the causes which impel them to the Separation.

—*The Declaration of Independence*

The Declaration of Independence is the principal document that defines and commemorates the birth of the United States and the independence of our nation. It defines the right of a people to defy the established order, to change their government, and to throw off a foreign oppressor. Perhaps

The Declaration of Independence articulates the birth of the United States as a free, independent nation. Today the document stands as a symbol of the principles on which the country was founded.

most famously, it expresses the overall philosophy behind America's foundation and independence and the basic freedoms that this nation strives to embody, such as "life, liberty, and the pursuit of happiness." The Declaration of Independence was written in 1776, but its message is timeless and still relevant today.

Seeds of Independence

From the very beginning, the colonists who settled in America had freedom on their minds, but for different reasons. For some, America represented hope for economic independence and an opportunity to profit from one's own labors. For others, the country was a refuge from political and religious persecution. Still others desired the freedom of space that this new and open land could provide. To this day, America is thought of as the land of opportunity—a notion that began way back in the 1500s, when the English made their first attempts to establish a permanent American settlement.

In the earliest days of American history, Great Britain was very much an expanding empire, with land holdings located all around the world, from India to Africa. There was tremendous incentive for such expansion. Britain itself had become crowded and overpopulated. As an island, land was limited and quickly taken by the wealthy. Most individuals worked and lived on land that was not theirs. It was owned and controlled by others. As tenant farmers, there was no hope of ever rising above one's station. Even many wealthy individuals felt constrained by the existing system of land ownership.

Still, it is hard for modern-day travelers to understand how anyone would want to undertake a sea voyage of many months from England to remote places, such as India or America. The trip certainly was not pleasant. Ships were often in poor condition. The seas were rough and, unlike today's ships, passengers felt every motion of the waves. Techniques for navigation were very primitive. Food was in short supply and often of poor quality, and many travelers came down with scurvy, a deadly disease caused by lack of vitamin C. People often did not survive such journeys.

Travel was a risk, but if successful the payoff could be great. For example, British businessmen who landed in India found an inexpensive and reliable source of tea, which their countrymen and women back home drank as part of their daily social routine. When news spread of the discovery of America, with its forests and coastal areas rich in natural resources, many British citizens no doubt saw a beacon of hope and opportunity. A wealthy gentleman farmer with a land grant from the king might grow very rich in America exporting tobacco back to England.

Corporate Colonies

Financial opportunities drew the first group of British travelers. In the seventeenth and eighteenth centuries, "companies" founded settlements. These were groups of businesspeople who had received royal charters from the English king to colonize those American lands over which England claimed ownership. Some interested parties stayed in England and bought stock in the company, hoping to see a future gain from their investment. Others both invested money and pledged themselves to live and work in America. The king would grant to such companies an exclusive monopoly to exploit a particular geographical area.

In 1606, two companies succeeded in establishing settlements in the New World: the Virginia Company of London and the Virginia Company of Plymouth. They were also commonly known as the London Company and the Plymouth Company. While the settlement at Jamestown in Virginia eventually failed, the settlement at Plymouth in Massachusetts endured.

These companies were an extension of British rule in the new land, with much of the profits and goods going back to the mother country. But over time those who had settled permanently in America began to perceive themselves as a community as much as a corporation, with a need to establish rules for living together that went beyond the mere extraction of profits. These groups underwent an evolution from corporation to colony. They had to establish local governments and to devise ways of making decisions that would be acceptable to people who regarded themselves as free British citizens.

When other corporate colonies found success in the New World, Britain tightened its reign in an attempt to maintain control and to benefit from the now profitable trade between the two places. In 1624, most of the American settlements were required to become royal colonies, with the English king presiding over them. This would be the beginning of a long struggle between the colonists and the mother country over who would be the main beneficiary of the increased trade.

Traveling from England to America was a treacherous and sometimes deadly experience. Still, the risk was worth it for those hoping for opportunities in the New World.

In Search of Religious Freedom

Another group interested in coming to America consisted of those people who had suffered from religious persecution. The kings and queens of Europe believed that their right to rule was ordained by God, and therefore their power was intimately connected to the established religion. After the Reformation, however, Puritans, Separatists, and other religious groups, who in one way or another worshipped their god directly and therefore represented a challenge to the state's authority over them, were ridiculed or persecuted in England and throughout Europe. In 1604, the archbishop of Canterbury cracked down on what the monarchy viewed as dissenters. Separatists, for example, were subjected to punishment.

In his account from that time, William Bradford, a governor of the Plymouth Colony who had come over on the *Mayflower*, wrote that Separatists "were taken and clapped up in prison, others had their houses beset and watched night and day . . . and the most were fain to flee and leave their houses and habitations, and the means of their livelihood."[1] The Pilgrims who had established the colony at Plymouth were Separatists.

In addition to Separatists, Quakers, Roman Catholics, French Huguenots, German Moravians, Jews from all over Europe, and other religious groups all sought safety and the freedom to practice their own religion in America. While written accounts suggest that these settlers had sentimental ties to their original homelands, they also possessed a thirst for freedom and self-rule.

Like many others who fled their homelands to pursue their religious beliefs without the threat of persecution, the Pilgrims were attracted to America's promise of freedom.

Opportunities for the Poor

The European aristocracy in the seventeenth and eighteenth centuries had left little room for the ambitions of self-made men and women. Descent from nobility, possession of land, and social class usually dictated a person's wealth and position in society. The New World represented opportunities for the poor to prosper or for men of energy to establish themselves. Here is a popular song of the day:

> *To such as to Virginia*
> *Do purpose to repair;*
> *And when that they shall hither come,*
> *Each man shall have his share,*
> *Day wages for the labourer,*
> *And for his more content,*
> *A house and garden plot shall have*
> *Besides 'tis further meant*
>
> *That every man shall have a post*
> *And not thereof denied*
> *Of general profit, as if that he*
> *Twelve pounds, ten shillings paid.*[2]

Poor families, and others seeking to improve their lives, came to America in droves, particularly in the eighteenth century when means of travel improved and the colonists had already firmly established cities and towns in the New World.

By 1700, the population of the English colonies in America was 250,000. In the next seventy-five years that figure jumped to 2 million. Often the poor were little better off when they arrived. Many came as indentured servants, contracted laborers who had to work for wealthier masters for a number of years before they could farm on their own. Tradesmen, mechanics, and others who had not been granted land in the New World had fewer political rights, repeating the patterns of disenfranchisement that existed in the old country. But the men of wealth and energy who established large estates and plantations in the colonies prospered and felt keenly how their profits were curtailed by the policies of the British government.

Colonial Government

Great Britain did what it could to maintain control over the colonies. The government within each colony was under the jurisdiction of a governor who was appointed by the English king. Each colony had a legislature and a court system, but both the king and the English Parliament reviewed and approved all the laws passed by colonial legislatures and courts. These officials had the power to reject colonial rulings that were felt to be contrary to English laws or interests. The colonists, of course, had no representatives in Parliament. Over the years, approximately 5 percent of all colonial laws were rejected, and the colonists did not take such decisions lightly. They resented the intrusion of the British monarchy into their lives, and they frequently appealed to the king and Parliament to reverse their decisions.

However, the growing population in the New World, the sheer distance between colony and mother country, and additional matters such as England's political disputes with other European powers prevented it from maintaining too strong a hold over the colonies. As a result, the colonies were able to develop their own government institutions. All of the colonies, except for Pennsylvania, had bicameral (two-house) legislatures resembling today's House of Representatives and Senate. Colonial voters could even elect lower house members.

Colonists actively participated in their local governments. Most colonists felt that it was their duty and their right to attend their local towns' meetings. Anything that would impact the lives of the community was discussed. This included matters ranging from military issues to bridge building to tax collecting to relations with Native Americans.

The Economical Disadvantages of the Colonies

When the colonists first arrived in the New World, they barely survived. Harsh weather, particularly in the New England region, reduced the yield of their crops. Starvation and disease were widespread. There was competition with Native Americans for land rights and resources, which often led to bloody wars. As time passed, however, life improved for the colonists and so did the economy. By the 1700s, a number of profitable industries had been established. These included farming, fishing and whaling, lumbering, iron making, and shipbuilding. In fact, middle Atlantic colonies such as Delaware were so fertile in their production of wheat and other grains that they became known as the bread colonies.

England's economic system at this time was dominated by the philosophy of mercantilism. Instead of policies of free trade, the English limited the importing of goods that would compete with those produced by their own industries. It was the role of the colonies to supply the mother country with raw materials, such as iron and lumber and

The excitement at arriving in the New World soon turned to frustration for many colonists, who struggled under England's unbalanced trade restrictions.

agricultural products. In return, the colonies were expected to buy finished manufactures from England. The labor applied to finished manufactures made them much more valuable and expensive than the raw materials supplied by the colonies, and this on top of arbitrary taxes placed on finished goods put the colonists at a disadvantage.

In modern terms, we would say that the balance of trade favored England, and the flow of wealth went toward England, not the colonies. The colonists had to export more and more raw materials in order to afford England's finished goods. American products became less valuable in relation to English exports.

This imbalance of economies began to fall apart over time. It became increasingly difficult for the colonies to export enough raw materials to survive. However, not everyone struggled. Some industries thrived. But even then, resentment against England for what seemed like a rigged system began to build. Many colonists were exasperated by England's dominance, and they longed for independence.

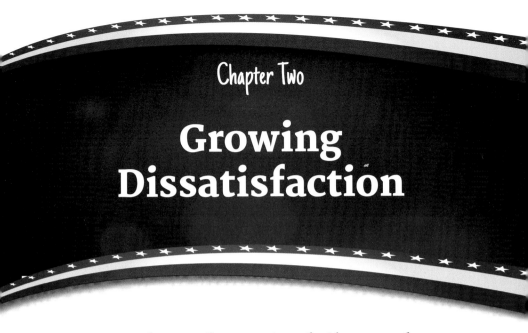

Chapter Two

Growing Dissatisfaction

But when a long train of Abuses and Usurpations, pursuing invariably the same Object, evinces a Design to reduce them under absolute Despotism, it is their Right, it is their Duty, to thrown off such Government, and to provide new Guards for their future Security.

—The Declaration of Independence

As the colonists grew increasingly dissatisfied with their arrangement with England, they actively traded with other countries in Europe, Africa, and the West Indies. But the British, who insisted on maintaining all control over its colonies, had trouble regulating America's trade. At American ports, where Britain relied on collecting hefty taxes from colonial trade, ships often slipped through without paying legal duties. In addition, many colonists engaged in smuggling, an way for them to avoid taxes and also spite the British.

The Navigation Acts and Other Prohibitions

These trade regulations were embodied in a series of laws known as the Navigation Acts. Desiring further control over the growing prosperity of colonial trade, the English Parliament passed these laws to protect British interests in the New World and to enrich the mother country. The trend toward heightened control began in 1645, with a law that prohibited imported whale oil from entering England unless it was shipped in an English vessel manned by English sailors. Whale oil in the seventeenth century was a very valuable and useful commodity. Oil lamps provided much of the light within homes and in public areas. Colonists actively hunted whales at that time, particularly off the New England coast, so this law limited their profits from exporting whale oil to England.

The first Navigation Act was passed in 1651, when Oliver Cromwell ruled England. It called for all products that entered England from the colonies to be shipped in British vessels with crews that were at least 75 percent English. The second Navigation Act was passed in 1660. It stated that all tobacco,

Oliver Cromwell (1599–1658) is touted as one of the greatest leaders in modern European history. Cromwell was a leader in England's Protestant Revolution and fought for freedom of religion and other civil liberties.

sugar, cotton, and wool grown in the colonies must be shipped exclusively to England and could not be sold directly to other European countries. Heavy taxes were imposed on these goods as well. The laws were immediately protested in the colonies. The only thing that made them tolerable was that they were difficult for the British to enforce. But England's inability to enforce the acts bred even more contempt for Parliament on the part of the colonists.

In 1663, another law was passed that affected goods coming into the New World. This act required that all foreign goods be shipped to England first before going to the colonies. In 1672, another law was passed that prohibited direct trade between the colonies themselves. If a colony such as Massachusetts wished to trade with Pennsylvania or any other colony, the goods would first have to be shipped to England and then back again. Other British laws imposed severe restrictions on colonial economic activity. The Corn Laws, first instituted around 1666 and designed to protect British farmers, prohibited American farmers from shipping their grain to England.

The British also tried to suppress the development of manufacturing in the colonies.

In 1732 an act of Parliament forbade the export of American-made hats to England or the rest of Europe, or from one colony to another. This was very damaging to colonial weavers and fur traders, at that time concentrated in the colony of New York. In 1750, Parliament prohibited the construction of forges, furnaces, and mills for the manufacture of iron goods.

Dissent over these laws quickly grew in the colonies, especially the northern ones, among the merchants, traders, and craftsmen. These laws not only were responsible for economic losses, but also were seen as unwarranted attempts to interfere with the rights of free Englishmen. Through local newspapers and at town hall meetings, the anger and resentment of the colonists toward the British monarchy and Parliament began to spread.

Smuggling

Because all these laws were difficult to enforce, the colonists continued to trade with other nations. Smuggling flourished. A highly profitable trade had developed with the West Indies, which sold sugar and molasses to the colonies. These sweeteners were mostly used to make rum. In 1733, Parliament imposed a tax on all molasses that came from non-British sources. Whereas islands such as

Barbados and Jamaica belonged to England, many other sources were considered "foreign" and were heavily taxed. The colonists initially protested the ruling, but when that failed they simply resorted to smuggling again.

The Sugar Act followed in 1764. This law was meant to replace the unpopular and virtually unenforceable Molasses Act. The new act did lower the duties on molasses, but raised the tax on sugar. It

The Sugar Act was enacted to impose strict taxes on sugar imported into the colonies. Britain's restrictive tax laws only encouraged smuggling.

also added a tax on Madeira wine that was imported into the colonies and added stricter regulations on all imported items. It also generated a great deal of protest and an increase in colonial smuggling. In fact, the needs of the smugglers actually had the effect of promoting the New England shipbuilding industry. To the great frustration of the British, colonial juries simply refused time and again to find smugglers guilty, in spite of the evidence against them.

Formation of the Sons of Liberty

The English were not the only colonial power in North America. The French had settled in Canada, and beginning in the late 1740s they began to move south into the upper Ohio Valley, just west of the English colonies, threatening to cut off the westward expansion of the English colonists. The colonists protested to the mother country, and during the 1750s and early 1760s a series of wars, called the French and Indian Wars, were fought to drive the French out of the Ohio Valley.

In 1765, to help pay for the French and Indian Wars, Parliament passed the Stamp Act. It required that colonists buy stamps for all printed items such as deeds, mortgages, business licenses, almanacs, newspapers, and even playing cards. Practically everyone in the colonies strongly opposed the Stamp Act. Underground groups called the Sons of Liberty formed to take action against this tax. Protests and demonstrations were organized. The stamps were burned and the tax collectors were threatened. Men such as Samuel Adams and James Otis were behind these new patriotic societies and urged members to take more violent action. In the House of Burgesses, Virginia's colonial legislature, Patrick Henry urged the passage of resolutions stating that only the local legislature had the right to tax Virginians. A popular slogan began to circulate through the colonies: "No taxation without representation."[1]

In August 1765, in protest against the Stamp Act, a Boston mob attacked the home of the chief justice of Massachusetts, Thomas Hutchinson, who was forced to flee for his life. Shortly afterward, in October, several delegates from each of the colonies met in New York City to form a general congress that asked the king to repeal the Stamp Act. Colonists refused to pay for the stamps, and most business and legal transactions came to a halt, since the documents authorizing them ceased to be prepared or printed.

At Virginia's House of Burgesses, Patrick Henry delivered a stunning oratory against Britain's Stamp Act.

Taxation Reaches a Breaking Point

The British believed that these acts of taxation were fair and appropriate. After all, the colonists had wanted British protection during the French and Indian Wars. King George III expressed his view of how British citizens, including colonists, should behave:

> *The obligation of each Briton to fulfill the political duties, receive a vast accession of strength when he calls to mind of what a noble and well balanced constitution of government he has the honour to belong; a constitution of free and equal laws, secured against arbitrary will and popular license, a constitution in fine the nurse of heroes, the parent of liberty, the patron of learning and the arts, and the dominion of laws.*[2]

The colonists, on the other hand, found fault with the system, particularly as it related to American life and business. Benjamin Franklin wrote:

> *Here numberless and needless places, enormous salaries, pensions, perquisites, bribes, groundless quarrels, foolish expeditions, false accounts or no accounts, contracts and jobs, devour all revenue, and produce continual necessity in the midst of natural plenty.*[3]

King George III (1738–1820) defeated France for power in North America but soon lost his colonies in the Revolutionary War.

Instead of trying to appease Franklin and the other colonists, the British reacted by passing yet another series of laws called the Townshend Acts in 1767. This time new duties were placed on imports of glass, paper, dyes, and tea. The colonists protested by boycotting these products. Eventually Parliament backed down by repealing the Townshend Acts, eliminating taxes on everything but tea, but not before a violent event shook the colonies.

Protests Lead to the Massacre

On the night of March 5, 1770, a group of protesters gathered to harass some British soldiers who were guarding Boston's Customs House. These soldiers, nicknamed redcoats or lobsterbacks by the colonists, were poorly paid members of the British army who had been put on duty as surrogate policemen. Words were exchanged between the two groups, and the protesters hurled some objects at the British. The fight escalated to the point where the British called for additional support.

More British soldiers came to the area. Chaos ensued. Without any apparent orders, the soldiers fired shots into the crowd, killing five of the young men. News of what came to be called the Boston Massacre spread throughout the colonies. Paul Revere, a popular silversmith and engraver, made an

The Boston Massacre escalated the ill will between the American colonists and Britain. The event generated propaganda that stirred colonists' desire for liberty.

engraving that immortalized the killings. It showed five small, black coffins surrounding a tribute to the young men. Families throughout the colonies hung copies of the engraving up in their kitchens, which served to remind them of the perceived British tyranny.

The Tea Party

Parliament had not repealed the tax on imported tea. The tax was meant to aid the financially troubled East India Company, a British company that specialized in the trading of tea, which then was one of the most popular beverages. Even with the tax, the East India tea was much less expensive than other teas available to the colonists. The colonists, however, were unwilling to accept any form of British taxation, for fear that one tax could lead to others in the future.

Ships carrying the British tea were docked in Boston harbor. The colonists boycotted the tea and called for the ships to leave. Massachusetts's governor Thomas Hutchinson refused to honor the demand. On the evening of December 16, 1773, a group of about 150 men disguised as Mohawk Indians boarded the ships and hurled the tea into the harbor. While the identity of the men remains largely unknown, it is believed that Samuel Adams led the group and gave the signal for the men to take action.

Punishment With the Coercive Acts

The British, including the prime minister, Lord Frederick North, were outraged by this destruction of property. In 1774, Parliament passed what came to be called by the colonists the Coercive Acts or Intolerable Acts, which were meant both to punish

THE DESTRUCTION OF TEA AT BOSTON HARBOR.

The Boston Tea Party was a shocking act of defiance against Britain. In response to the organized protest, Britain unwisely passed more punishing acts.

the people of Massachusetts and to control them more effectively.

The first act, called the Boston Port Act, closed Boston's harbor to all shipping. It was only to be opened when Boston residents agreed to formally apologize to the British and pay for the lost tea. The second act, the Administration of Justice Act, stated that British officers or soldiers who were arrested for murder in the colonies had to be returned to England for trial. The third act, the Massachusetts Government Act, gave to the colonial governors

Lord Frederick North (1732–1792) served as prime minister to King George III. Perhaps because of his tone deaf insistence on passing the Coercive Acts, North is generally considered responsible for losing the American colonies.

the power to appoint all local officials, severely curtailing the authority of the colonial legislatures, and also required that all local town meetings were illegal unless the governor granted prior permission. The fourth act, the Quartering Act, ordered the colonists to feed and provide shelter in their homes to British soldiers. The final act, the Quebec Act, returned large tracts of land west of the Appalachian Mountains to the French. This reversed the results of the French and Indian Wars, curtailed the westward expansion of the colonists, and threatened them with renewed war with the Indians and their French allies.

The Coercive Acts had an effect on the colonists that was opposite of what Parliament intended. Instead of pushing them back into submission, it stoked the fires of the growing movement for independence among the colonies. As a result, they became united and strong.

In 1774, an organized group of patriots representing each colony except Georgia met in Philadelphia to discuss their mounting frustration with the British, particularly the Intolerable Acts. This group would become known as the Continental Congress. Their historic sessions would sow the seeds of independence from Britain.

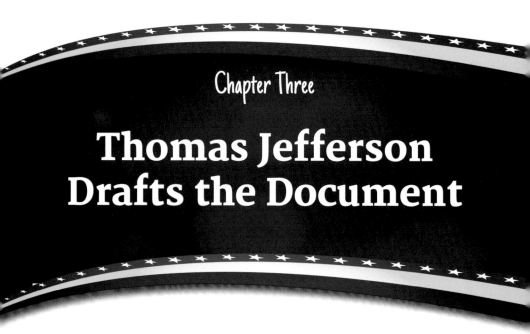

Chapter Three

Thomas Jefferson Drafts the Document

In every stage of these Oppressions we have Petitioned for Redress in the most humble Terms: Our repeated Petitions have been answered only by repeated Injury. A Prince, whose Character is thus marked by every act which may define a Tyrant, is unfit to be the Ruler of a free People.

—The Declaration of Independence

Among the delegates present at the First Continental Congress was a patriot who would greatly influence the course of America's history, Thomas Jefferson. Born in Shadwell, Virginia, on April 13, 1743, Thomas Jefferson was forced to grow up quickly. He had six sisters and one brother; two other brothers had died while still infants. He was brought up in the lap of luxury, surrounded

Thomas Jefferson was the primary drafter of the Declaration of Independence. Jefferson would become the nation's first secretary of state before holding the titles of vice president and president.

by pursuits such as horseback riding and music. His boyhood ended, however, when at the age of fourteen, his father died. Jefferson, being the eldest son in the family, inherited the family estate. It included 2,500 acres (10 km²) of land and at least twenty slaves. A guardian managed the estate until Jefferson was twenty-one years old.

By most accounts, young Jefferson was not very close to his mother. He did, however, greatly admire his charismatic father. Born into a lower middle-class family, Peter Jefferson worked hard to acquire his estate, to rise up in the social ranks in Virginia, and to become a member of the House of Burgesses. He died as perhaps the most respected individual of his time in the colony. He laid open a path to success for his son and instilled in him the virtues of education, hard work, and a love for the new country.

Thomas Jefferson entered William and Mary College in Virginia in 1760. There he befriended two men, William Small and George Wythe, both of whom would greatly influence Jefferson's later views. Small was a mathematics professor who was very interested in all of the sciences, and he believed that scientific and rational principles could be used to understand the world order, that is, its history and political development as well as that of the world of nature. This point of view, which developed during the European Enlightenment in the century before the French Revolution, was in opposition to the views of the British monarchy and its supporters, men like Edmund Burke. They believed that kings held their power from God and that this authority could not be questioned. Wythe was a respected lawyer in Virginia. He, along with Small, introduced Jefferson to Governor Francis Fauquier and other powerful men and politicians within the colony.

Jefferson and the Continental Congress

Inspired by his father and his college friends, Jefferson embarked on a political career. He was elected to the House of Burgesses in 1769. The young statesman proved himself to be a talented writer. His clear, simple, yet impassioned style greatly impressed his colleagues, so that whenever a law or resolution needed to be drafted, young Jefferson was often called. It is not surprising, then, that Jefferson found himself a delegate to the First Continental Congress that met in Philadelphia in May 1774, to discuss what to do about the oppressive acts of the British government.

That Congress adjourned in late October of 1774 without agreeing on any unified policy for the colonies, but the delegates agreed to meet again in a Second Continental Congress in Philadelphia in May 1775. Between the two Congresses, events came to a head. In April, British troops from Boston, attempting to seize arms stored by the colonists, were fired upon and driven back at the battles of Lexington and Concord. The Massachusetts colonists were now in open rebellion against Britain.

The Second Continental Congress convened on May 5, 1775. Among the delegates were George Washington, John Adams, Samuel Adams, Patrick Henry, Benjamin Franklin, Richard Henry Lee, Benjamin Harrison, and John Hancock. There was still much division of opinion about what to do. Though they objected to the taxes on colonial trade and manufacture, many delegates still felt a strong loyalty to the mother country.

War Erupts in the Colonies

On June 17, colonists and British troops again clashed at the Battle of Bunker Hill north of the city of Boston, and on that same day the delegates in Philadelphia chose George Washington as commander of the Continental Army. The delegates passed a resolution known as the Declaration of Causes of Taking Up Arms, which listed the reasons the colonists believed that Britain was the aggressor

The British won the Battle of Bunker Hill, but their considerable losses gave the colonial soldiers an important boost of confidence that would help them throughout the war.

and why they felt they had the right to form their own army. At the same time they tried desperately to avoid war. Delegate John Dickinson wrote the Olive Branch Petition, an appeal directly to King George III with suggestions on how to resolve the disputes between the colonies and England. Believing the Continental Congress to be an illegal and rebellious assembly, the king would not even read the petition.

British intransigence was pushing the delegates closer and closer to a resolution of independence. With his rejection of Dickinson's appeal, the king had effectively declared the colonies to be in open rebellion, and by the second half of 1775, the American Revolution was underway.

After several months of fighting, delegate Richard Henry Lee of Virginia submitted a resolution to the Second Continental Congress called the Declaration of Rights of the Colonies. It declared that "these United Colonies are, and of right ought to be, free and independent States, that they are absolved from all allegiances to the British Crown, and that all political connection between them and the State of Great Britain is, and ought to be, totally dissolved."[1]

Lee's resolution formally declared American independence. However, the delegates felt that a

John Dickinson (1732–1808) penned the Olive Branch Petition, an attempt to negotiate with Britain. Dickinson's ideas were rejected by the king.

more eloquent and dramatic document was needed to explain their decision not only to all the residents of the colonies, but to the rest of the world. The rulers of other European countries, though they may have had grievances against England, still might not be keen to accept the idea of rebellion as a natural right of oppressed people. It was crucial for the colonists to forge some alliances with the European powers in this struggle. They wanted as well to preserve and strengthen trade with Europe, considering the break with England. So in June 1775, the Continental Congress appointed a committee to draft another document explaining the American cause.

Drafting the Declaration of Independence

Five men were appointed to the committee. They were Roger Sherman, Robert Livingston, John Adams, Benjamin Franklin, and Thomas Jefferson. Sherman had earned the respect of his colleagues in Connecticut, but held fairly conservative political views. Livingston was also rather conservative, but both he and Sherman's appointments were intentional, as not all of the colonists wanted immediate revolution. Adams was a well-known politician and writer. Franklin was a bit of everything, a popular and well-liked speaker, an inventor, a writer, and a scientist.

Jefferson was the youngest and least experienced of these men. His selection for the committee was something of a last-minute decision. His friend George Wythe was the expected choice, but Wythe declined. Richard Henry Lee was another possible choice for the committee, since he had written the formal resolution of independence in the first place. However, Lee's hardline views clashed with the

Roger Sherman, Robert Livingston, Benjamin Franklin, John Adams, and Thomas Jefferson were selected by the Continental Congress to draft the Declaration of Independence.

more conservative colonists. Also, Lee's wife was ill at the time, and other business matters required his attention in Williamsburg. Furthermore, Jefferson initially did not want to be a part of the committee. Virginia was in the process of writing its first constitution, and Jefferson thought that this would be a much more important and exciting challenge for him. Almost by default, Jefferson was chosen to be the committee's fifth and final man.

Accounts differ as to how Jefferson was picked to write the Declaration of Independence, among the other four men. In his diary Jefferson simply wrote, "The committee for drawing the Declaration of Independence desired me to do it."[2] John Adams provides a slightly more dramatic account. In his letters, Adams wrote that Jefferson "proposed to me to make the draft, I said I will not; You shall do it. Oh no! Why will you not? You ought to do it. I will not. Why? Reasons enough. What can be your reasons? Reason 1st. You are a Virginian and a Virginian ought to appear at the head of this business. Reason 2nd. I am obnoxious, suspected and unpopular; you are very much otherwise. Reason 3rd. You can write ten times better than I can. 'Well,' said Jefferson, 'if you are decided I will do as well as I can.' Very well, when you have drawn it up we will have a meeting."[3]

By the Second Continental Congress, John Adams (1735–1826) was radically in favor of independence. He became the congress's central figure.

The men met in private to discuss what should be stated in the document. Jefferson listened intently and took careful notes. Over the next two weeks, he used his superior writing talents to craft a document that reflected the committees' ideas. On June 28, 1775, Jefferson submitted his first draft of the Declaration of Independence.

Chapter Four

No Original Ideas

We have warned them from Time to Time of Attempts by their Legislature to extend an unwarrantable Jurisdiction over us. We have reminded them of the Circumstances of our Emigration and Settlement here. We have appealed to their native Justice and Magnanimity, and we have conjured them by the Ties of our common Kindred to disavow these Usurpations, which would inevitably interrupt our Connections and Correspondence. They too have been deaf to the Voice of Justice and Consanguinity.

—*The Declaration of Independence*

Although the Declaration of Independence reflected the ideas of the drafting committee and the colonies' delegates, it was very much a product of Thomas Jefferson's beliefs. Thus, it is extraordinary that the document is read, even today, as a universal statement of human rights. A gifted writer, Jefferson had honed his radical ideas regarding independence two years earlier as author of the instructions for Virginia's delegates to the First Continental Congress. When it came time to write the Declaration of Independence, he knew exactly how to approach it.

To devise an argument that would explain the colonists' dissent, but not make them all seem like rebels against the crown, Jefferson redefined the nature and powers of kingship. He wrote that the monarch "is no more than the chief officer of the people appointed by the laws, and circumscribed with definite powers, to assist in working the great machine of government, erected for their use, and consequently subject to their superintendence."[1] This view almost anticipates our conception of the American president today. The president holds power to help govern the people, but he is responsible to the people, who have the right to remove him if necessary. Jefferson began with the principle of the sovereignty of the people and abandoned the notion that kings held their power by divine and unquestionable right. Jefferson wrote that "our ancestors, before their emigration to America, were the free inhabitants of the British dominions in Europe, and possessed a right which nature has given to all men, of departing from the country in which chance, not choice, has placed them, of going in quest of new habitations, and of there establishing new societies, under such laws and regulations as to them shall seem most likely to promote public happiness."[2]

The argument was a clever one. Jefferson had formulated a claim that the colonies had always enjoyed personal and political freedoms. It was only after they created settlements in the New World that they agreed, of their own free will, to recognize the authority of the king. With a few slight changes, this was to become a central concept of the Declaration of Independence.

Jefferson's Influences

A few members of the drafting committee, upon reading Jefferson's work, commented that he had not written anything new, that all of the ideas mentioned in the document had been stated before using almost the same choice of words. John Adams, for example, wrote of the Declaration of Independence in 1822, saying, "There is not an idea in it but what had been hackneyed in Congress for two years before."[3] It should be noted, however, that

Adams felt a twinge of jealousy over the widespread admiration for the document and the fame that it afforded Jefferson. Many scholars believe that Adams, as one of the senior members of the drafting committee, regretted not having written the document himself once he became aware of its future historical significance.

Still, there is some truth in what Adams said. The Declaration of Independence put forth ideas that the colonists had been discussing for some time, ideas that had been put forward by many European writers and thinkers. Jefferson himself admitted this. In a letter to Richard Henry Lee dated May 8, 1825, only a year before his death, Jefferson wrote that he intentionally borrowed from others:

> *. . . with respect to our rights, and the acts of the British government contravening those rights, there was but one opinion on this side of the water. All American whigs thought alike on these subjects. When forced, therefore, to resort to arms for redress, an appeal to the tribunal of the world was deemed proper for our justification. This was the object of the Declaration of Independence. Not to find out new principles, or new arguments, never before thought of, not merely to say things which had never been said before; but to place before mankind the common sense of the subject,*

Richard Henry Lee (1732–1794) called for independence from Britain during the Second Continental Congress. Lee became president of the Continental Congress and a US senator.

*in terms so plain and firm as to command
their assent, and to justify ourselves in the
independent stand we are compelled to take.
Neither aiming at originality of principle or
sentiment, nor yet copied from any particular
and previous writing, it was intended to be an
expression of the American mind, and to give
to that expression the proper tone and spirit
called for by the occasion. All its authority rests
then on the harmonizing sentiments of the day,
whether expressed in conversation, in letters,
printed essays, or in the elementary books of
public right, as Aristotle, Cicero, Locke, Sidney,
etc.*[4]

Being a learned man who greatly enjoyed
literature and philosophy, Jefferson most certainly
would have been familiar with all of the writings of
the above mentioned men, but one in particular,
John Locke, seemed to inspire Jefferson when he
wrote the Declaration of Independence.

John Locke

John Locke was a seventeenth-century English
philosopher. Nearly a decade before Jefferson
drafted the Declaration of Independence, Locke
wrote a book entitled *Two Treatises of Civil
Government.* Locke's position was not that different
from Jefferson's. British subjects were unhappy with

the state of the monarchy and decided to revolt against King James II, who promoted Catholicism in a largely Protestant country and who had challenged the rights of Parliament to limit his power. The so-called Glorious Revolution of 1688 brought William of Orange and his wife Mary to the English throne as joint sovereigns pledged to defend English liberties and Protestantism. Locke and those who supported the revolution felt compelled to explain their cause to the world.

Locke wanted to dispel the notion that kings and queens ruled by divine right. In order to do this, he had to demonstrate that men possessed natural rights and freedoms and that monarchs held their power with the consent of free men. Locke also wanted to present a framework for a different political system, one that would give the people more of a voice in how they were governed. The second chapter of Locke's book, "Of the State of Nature," must have been of particular interest to Jefferson, because many of its ideas can be found in the Declaration of Independence.

Locke began by describing free will as a fundamental state of nature. By this he meant that all people are born with a certain amount of freedom to think, speak, and do as they see fit. Nature, however,

The writings of English philosopher John Locke (1632–1704), particularly his views on personal rights and liberties, strongly influenced Thomas Jefferson as he drafted the Declaration of Independence.

is not in a state of complete chaos, with everyone doing exactly what he or she wants to do. Locke wrote that "The state of Nature has a law of Nature to govern it, which obliges every one, and reason, which is that law, teaches all mankind who will but consult it, that being all equal and independent, no one ought to harm another in his life, health, liberty, or possessions . . ."[5] Locke was saying that whereas nature made man free, it also gave him the power of reason, and reason imposed moral law on men and required them to act in a certain way toward each other.

Locke strengthens this point later by writing, "Every one as he is bound to preserve himself, and not to quit his station willfully, so by the like of reason, when his own preservation comes not in competition, ought he as much as he can to preserve the rest of mankind, and not unless it be to do justice on an offender, take away or impair the life, or what tends to the preservation of the life, the liberty, health, limb, or goods of another."[6] Locke did not mention "the pursuit of happiness," but his vision of life and liberty certainly influenced Jefferson, who worked Locke's phrasing into the Declaration of Independence.

George Mason

Another influence on Jefferson was the Virginia Declaration of Rights. This document was written by George Mason and was adopted by the Virginia Constitutional Convention on June 12, 1776, just a few days before Jefferson began his draft of the Declaration of Independence. In the letter to Richard Henry Lee in 1825, Jefferson wrote, "That George Mason was the author of the bill of rights, and the constitution founded on it, the evidence of the day established fully in my mind."[7] The Declaration of Independence borrowed heavily from the document. This is particularly evident when we examine the Virginia Declaration's first three sections:

> *Section 1. That all men are by nature equally free and independent and have certain inherent rights, of which, when they enter into a state of society, they cannot, by any compact, deprive or divest their posterity; namely, the enjoyment of life and liberty, with the means of acquiring and possessing property, and pursuing and obtaining happiness and safety.*

> *Section 2. That all power is vested in, and consequently derived from, the people; that magistrates are their trustees and servants and at all times amenable to them.*

George Mason (1725–1792) also influenced Jefferson's draft of the Declaration of Independence. Jefferson borrowed heavily from Mason's Virginia Declaration of Rights.

> *Section 3. That government is, or ought to be, instituted for the common benefit, protection, and security of the people, nation, or community; of all the various modes of government, that is best which is capable of producing the greatest degree of happiness and safety and is most effectively secured against the danger of maladministration. And that, when any government shall be found inadequate or contrary to these purposes, a majority of the community has an indubitable, inalienable, and indefeasible right to reform, alter, or abolish it, in such manner as shall be judged most conducive to the public weal.*[8]

Mason's influential document helped to inspire political leaders in the other colonies when they too drafted each of their states' constitutions. In addition to its direct contribution to the Declaration of Independence, the Virginia Declaration of Rights later influenced yet another important American document, the Bill of Rights. George Mason, a Virginia statesman, held liberal democratic views and was strongly against slavery long before it was popular to hold this belief. While his name is not as well known as that other politicians of his time, Mason, in his authorship of the Virginia Declaration of Rights, was one of America's most influential figures in creating a vision of what America was and could be.

Thomas Paine

John Locke helped to shape Jefferson's view of life and government, and George Mason gave him the foundation for expressing these views, but it was Thomas Paine, a thirty-nine-year-old radical journalist and essayist, who added a fiery determination and a sense of purpose to Jefferson's work. In January of 1776, Paine published a pamphlet entitled *Common Sense*, in which he argued that separation from England was inevitable and that governments ought to represent their citizens and to interfere in the lives of those citizens as little as possible. *Common Sense* cost two shillings and sold more than half a million copies.

In the pages of *Common Sense*, Paine expressed with a burning passion what was on the minds of many of the colonists. He criticized the monarchy, again brought forth the notion of the natural rights of man as previously described by Locke, and, perhaps most important, justified the creation of a free and independent American republic. The language was fiery, dramatic, and uncompromising:

> *But where says some is the King of America?*
> *I'll tell you Friend, he reigns above, and doth*

Thomas Paine (1737–1809) inspired the colonists to revolt from England. He also wrote a pamphlet defending the French Revolution.

not make havoc of mankind like the Royal of Britain. Yet that we may not appear to be defective even in earthly honours, let a day be solemnly set apart for proclaiming the charter; let it be brought forth placed on the divine law, the word of God; let a crown be placed thereon, by which the world may know, that so far as we approve of monarchy, that in America THE LAW IS KING.

For as in absolute governments the King is law, so in free countries the law ought to be King; and there ought to be no other. But lest any ill use should afterwards arise, let the crown at the conclusion of the ceremony be demolished, and scattered among the people whose right it is.

A government of our own is our natural right: And when a man seriously reflects on the precariousness of human affairs, he will become convinced, that it is infinitely wiser and safer, to form a constitution of our own in a cool and deliberate manner, while we have it in our power, than to trust such an interesting event to time and chance.[9]

Common Sense had tremendous influence on Jefferson—not only in its ideas but in its reception by the public. When Jefferson first read the pamphlet, before its publication, he was dazzled. However, he wondered whether the colonists

Wolcott 6

PRIMARY SOURCE

PLAIN TRUTH;

ADDRESSED TO THE

INHABITANTS

O F

AMERICA,

Containing, Remarks

ON A LATE PAMPHLET,

entitled

COMMON SENSE:

Wherein are shewn, that the Scheme of INDEPENDENCE is Ruinous, Delusive, and Impracticable: That were the Author's Asseverations, Respecting the Power of AMERICA, as Real as Nugatory; Reconciliation on liberal Principles with GREAT BRITAIN, would be exalted Policy: And that circumstanced as we are, Permanent Liberty, and True Happiness, can only be obtained, by HONORABLE CONNECTIONS, with that Kingdom.

WRITTEN BY CANDIDUS.

Dock

Will ye turn from flattery, and attend to this Side. ?

There TRUTH, unlicenc'd, walks; and dares accost Even Kings themselves, the Monarchs of the Free! THOMSON on the Liberties of BRITAIN.

PHILADELPHIA:

Printed, and Sold, by R. BELL, in Third-Street.

MDCCLXXVI.

Thomas Paine published his 1776 pamphlet *Common Sense* anonymously. The document found a large readership and inspired colonists to break free from Britain.

would respond favorably to Paine's radical viewpoints. When *Common Sense* was published, it became overwhelmingly popular with the public. This popularity made Jefferson and the other members of the Continental Congress confident that the Declaration of Independence would be received in the same way. The colonists, it seemed, were ready to break free from Britain.

Chapter Five

The Final Document

We, therefore, the Representatives of the UNITED STATES OF AMERICA, in GENERAL CONGRESS, Assembled, appealing to the Supreme Judge of the World for the Rectitude of our Intentions, do, in the Name, and by Authority of the good People of these Colonies, solemnly Publish and Declare, That these United Colonies are, and of Right ought to be, FREE AND INDEPENDENT STATES; that they are absolved from all Allegiance to the British Crown, and that all political Connection between them and the State of Great Britain, is and ought to be totally dissolved, and that as FREE AND INDEPENDENT STATES, they have full Power to levy War, conclude Peace, contract Alliances, establish Commerce, and do all other Acts and Things which INDEPENDENT STATES may of right do.

—The Declaration of Independence

As with most important documents, Jefferson's first draft was not the Declaration of Independence we can read today. The document is Jefferson's, but not entirely so. Other members of the drafting committee, particularly Adams and Franklin, left their mark on the final document. Jefferson's initial draft was read, commented on, and edited by the drafting committee. After that it was reviewed by the Continental Congress, discussed and debated, and revised.

The second version is the declaration after the Continental Congress edited it. Congress felt a sense of urgency in making the document available to Americans as soon as possible. Right after Congress revised the committee's draft, it was sent to the printer John Dunlap. He received the copy late on the afternoon of July 4, 1776. By the following morning he had printed enough copies for the Congress and its various committees. Typesetting and printing in colonial times was a much slower process than it is now. Each individual letter had to be set into place by hand. When the typesetting was finished, the letters were inked and sheets of paper were hand-cranked over them. It is not certain how many copies Dunlap was able to print, but twenty-

Ben Franklin's contributions to Jefferson's draft of the Declaration of Independence were said to be small but significant.

two copies of this version of the declaration survive today.

The Official Declaration

The final official version of the Declaration of Independence bore the title "In CONGRESS, July 4th, 1776. The unanimous Declaration of the thirteen united STATES OF AMERICA." Today the phrase "United States" is part of our everyday language, but this was the first time that those words had ever appeared together in an official document. It brought great power to the declaration, suggesting that all the people were organized and of one mind in pursuit of independence.

This final copy was made upon the order of the Continental Congress to create a "fairly engrossed" version of the declaration. "Engrossing" means to copy an important document by hand in bold, clear lettering.[1] Engrossed documents are usually printed on parchment, paper made from animal skin. A Congressional assistant named Timothy Matlock is believed to have engrossed the declaration onto parchment. This is the document that is now on display at the National Archives in Washington DC.

Aside from these three official declarations, several other versions of the document exist. Congressional secretary Charles Thomson made a copy that shows certain corrections to Jefferson's draft. John Adams made a copy. Jefferson himself made another copy to send to his friend and colleague George Wythe. Jefferson made two additional copies for George Pendleton and James Madison. From these various copies it is possible to reconstruct the process by which the document was edited after the committee sent it to Congress.

The drafting committee, known as the Committee of Five, presented the revised declaration to Congress on June 28, 1776.

Today, using computers, writers can erase, move, and otherwise change documents with a few keystrokes, and the old version of a document disappears. The advantage, of course, is that this greatly speeds up the editing process. In the eighteenth century, however, writers had to correct everything by hand in pen. While laborious, this method provides historians and scholars with a clear view of what the original sentences looked like, who changed the wording (based on differences in handwriting, if the changes were not actually initialed), and what phrasing was decided upon for the final version.

Jefferson's Revisions

The rough draft shows a great deal of self-editing by Jefferson. He was known to be a slow and meticulous writer who chose his words carefully. For example, he originally wrote this as the first sentence of the Declaration of Independence:

> *When in the course of human events it becomes necessary for a people to advance from that subordination in which they have hitherto remained & to assume among the powers of the earth the equal and independent station to which the laws of nature and of nature's god entitle them, a decent respect to the opinions of*

mankind requires that they should declare the causes which impel them to change.[2]

Jefferson then changed this to read:

When in the course of human events it becomes necessary for one people to dissolve the political bands which have connected them with another, and to assume among the powers of the earth the separate and equal station to which the laws of nature and of nature's god entitle them, a decent respect to the opinions of mankind requires that they should declare the causes which impel them to the separation.[3]

Note how the changes emphasize the colonies' break with England. Jefferson cleverly acknowledges America's former "political bands" with England, but uses words like "dissolve" and "separation" to establish the colonies' newly acknowledged independence.

The next phrase, perhaps the most well known of the entire declaration, shows further editing by Jefferson. His first version read:

We hold these truths to be sacred & undeniable, that all Men are created equal & independent, that from that equal creation they derive in rights inherent and inalienable among which are the preservation of life, & liberty, & the pursuit of happiness . . .[4]

He then changed the phrase to read:

We hold these truths to be self-evident, that all Men are created equal, that they are endowed by their creator with inherent and inalienable rights; that among these are life & liberty, & the pursuit of happiness.

This time the revision not only tightens and clarifies the meaning, but communicates a sense that the colonists were, by right of birth, entitled to certain powers and freedoms. Jefferson himself made most of the major revisions to his initial version of the Declaration of Independence. Franklin and Adams must have liked what they read, or else they were pressed for time, because their changes are limited mostly to a few individual words. For example, Jefferson wrote "arbitrary power." Franklin changed this to "absolute Despotism," likely to provide more of a jolt to readers. In another instance, Jefferson wrote the word "majesty." Adams changed this to "king of Great Britain." Majesty implies a sense of respect and admiration that Adams and the colonists did not wish to encourage at this crucial time of separation with England. Yet another word change occurred closer to the end of the document. Jefferson wrote that England was sending Scottish and other foreign mercenaries over to the colonies to "invade & deluge us in blood." Franklin clarified the sentiment by changing it to read, "destroy us."[5]

Congressional Revisions

Congress took a much heavier hand in editing Jefferson's document. Throughout, the members added, changed, and excised numerous phrases, sentences, and entire sections. At least three changes radically departed from Jefferson's original draft. The first was the complete elimination of Jefferson's section accusing King George III of promoting slavery within the colonies. It had read:

He has incited treasonable insurrections of our fellow citizens, with the allurements of forfeiture & confiscation of our property. He has waged cruel war against human nature itself, violating its most sacred rights of life and liberty in the persons of a distant people who never offended him, captivating & carrying them into slavery in another hemisphere, or to incur miserable death in their transportation thither. This piratical warfare, the opprobrium of INFIDEL powers, is the warfare of the CHRISTIAN king of Great Britain. Determined to keep open a market where MEN should be bought & sold, he has prostituted his negative for suppressing every legislative attempt to prohibit or to restrain this execrable commerce. And that this assemblage of horrors might want no fact

*of distinguished die, he is now exciting those
very people to rise in arms among us, and to
purchase that liberty of which he has deprived
them, by murdering the people on whom he
also obtruded them: thus paying off former
crimes committed against the LIBERTIES of
one people, with crimes which he urges them to
commit against the LIVES of another.[6]*

The southern colonies, namely South
Carolina and Georgia, desired that the slave trade
continue. Their economies were based on slave
labor. Jefferson, though he owned his own slaves,
was against slavery in theory and became very
passionate when speaking or writing about the
subject. Nevertheless, the unity of the colonies in
their opposition to English domination was the
important issue for the Continental Congress, and
so this condemnation of slavery was removed from
the Declaration of Independence.

The second and third major changes were to
omit Jefferson's mention of "Scottish mercenaries"
and to lessen the overall criticism of the English
people. Congress did not wish to anger the
many Scottish individuals who had settled in the
colonies. They also wished to keep their argument
between the colonies and the king, not the English
commoners. Many Americans were English and

had close personal ties to England. There were also a number of Englishmen who were sympathetic to the American cause. By leaving Parliament and the British public out of the fight, they kept open the possibility of future trade and business relations between the two countries after independence.

Respecting Congress's wishes and desiring to move forward with the declaration, Jefferson agreed to the revisions. Privately, however, he thought that his initial document was much better than the changed version. In 1818, Jefferson downplayed the reasons given by Congress for the revisions in a letter:

> *When the Declaration of Independence was under the consideration of Congress, there were two or three unlucky expressions in it which gave offense to some members. The words "Scotch and other foreign auxiliaries" excited the ire of a gentleman or two of that country. Severe strictures on the conduct of the British King, in negativing our repeated repeals of the law which permitted the importation of slaves, were disapproved by some Southern gentleman, whose reflections were not yet matured to the full abhorrence of that traffic. Although the offensive expressions were immediately yielded, these gentlemen continued their depredations on other parts of the instrument.*[7]

Although he chafed at some of the suggested edits made to his writing, Jefferson's final document reflects compromise and a willingness to put aside his ego for the greater good. The document was something to be proud of, and it united American colonists, who were ready to stand on their own. On July 4, 1776, two days after voting for independence, the Continental Congress approved Jefferson's revised Declaration of Independence.

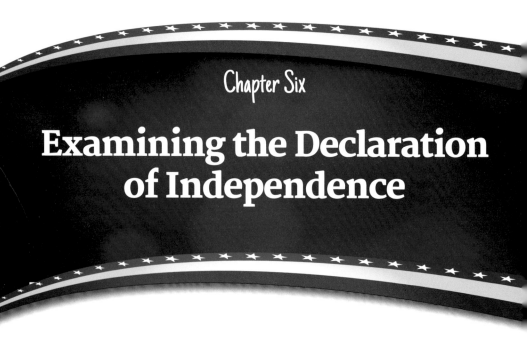

Chapter Six

Examining the Declaration of Independence

And for the support of this Declaration, with a firm Reliance on the Protection of divine Providence, we mutually pledge to each other our Lives, our Fortunes, and our sacred Honor.

—*The Declaration of Independence*

Just four days later, on July 8, 1776, Colonel John Nixon read the Declaration of Independence to a crowd of Philadelphia's citizens assembled at the Pennsylvania State House Yard. For the rest of the day, celebratory bells could be heard ringing throughout the city. Patriot Christopher Marshall wrote in his diary, "There were bonfires, ringing bells, and other great demonstrations of joy upon the unanimity of the Declaration."[1]

The next day, George Washington, commander of the Continental Army, read the Declaration to his troops. In the days and months to follow, news of the declaration spread throughout all of the colonies.

The Declaration of Independence can be divided into several distinct sections: a preamble and declaration of rights, a bill of indictment, and a statement of independence.

A year and half after reading the Declaration, George Washington and his troops would find themselves starving and freezing at Valley Forge in Pennsylvania during the Revolutionary War.

The Declaration's Introduction

Jefferson took the time to select the perfect words for the declaration's preamble. The first paragraph of the Declaration of Independence consists of one long sentence, written in a style that contemporaries of Jefferson referred to as "felicitous," or appropriate and effective. As many biographers of Jefferson have stated, he was not merely chronicling history, but making it.

Jefferson had to convince the rest of the world, and doubting Americans, that separation from England was the right and justifiable thing to do. Jefferson did this by drawing on currents of liberal European thought that asserted that man's freedom was a natural right. He was free because he was born free, not because he had been given that freedom by another person or institution—a king or a church. Such freedom was "inalienable," that is, it could not be taken away. Princes and monarchs had for centuries formed and broken alliances with each other, been subservient or rebelled against each other, but Jefferson was stating broader principles, that the power to govern itself derived from the consent of free individuals, that governments had to justify their actions to their citizens. If governments, or more to the point, the British government, could not do so, they could be cast aside by the people.

It is also important to note that the document espouses no particular religion. While religion was very much a part of the lives of most Americans in the eighteenth century, Jefferson and his colleagues recognized that many different religions already were being practiced in the colonies. If the Declaration of Independence was to appeal to all citizens of the United States, the wording had to embrace people of many different faiths.

The rights of life and liberty had been documented before by John Locke and other philosophers of the European Enlightenment, but Jefferson added a unique phrase, the "pursuit of Happiness." It called to mind contemporary theories about the nature and origin of government that were being debated by liberal democrats. Such theories stated that in a perfect world there would be no need for government. A perfect world is one in which all men are happy and free to live as they please. Since conditions are not perfect, given crime, disputes, factionalism, and other problems, government is required, but it should not impede an individual's freedom and the quest for a better life. Governments were subordinate to individuals in such theories.

The Declaration of Independence, however, also says that "governments long established should not be changed for light and transient causes . . ." Jefferson and the members of the Continental Congress were, after all, part of a government themselves. Foreseeing the need for a stable ruling body after the break with England, they were careful to suggest that governments should be respected, but not if they were to engage in a "long train of abuses . . ."

The Charges Against King George

Jefferson devoted the entire middle section of the Declaration of Independence to listing the charges against the king that impelled the colonists to take action. While the preamble is one of the most well-known paragraphs of any American historical document, this bill of indictment is not often quoted. The other sections of the declaration have a timeless quality about them and embody general principles that can apply to every American in any century. The bill of indictment, however, was very much linked to the specific policies of the English government.

The first charge, "He has refused his Assent to Laws, the most wholesome and necessary for the public good," referred to the king's power to veto laws decided upon by the colonial legislatures. Initially Britain stayed out of America's local lawmaking efforts, for the most part. But King George III took a heavier hand, which angered Americans. Jefferson was especially furious when the king prevented the colony of Virginia from curbing its slave trade.

The next eight charges cover a variety of issues of great concern to the colonists at the time. They involved Britain's prior actions relating to immigration within the New World, as well as legal matters and land rights. Initially, land was not very hard to obtain in the Americas, at least when compared to the situation in Europe. In 1773, the king approved a law that suspended the issuance of certain land rights. This alarmed the colonists, as it made it very difficult for the average frontier citizen to obtain his own home.

The tenth charge states, "He has erected a multitude of New Offices, and sent hither swarms of Officers to harass our people, and eat out their substance." This goes back to the acts of taxation in the seventeenth and eighteenth centuries. Many British officers were employed in the colonies to enforce these tax laws. The officers came to symbolize the hated taxes and were loathed and widely criticized by Americans, who felt that the officers abused their positions. The next few charges refer to similar complaints regarding the British military presence in the colonies.

The list then goes on to mention the trade and tax disputes more directly. This is evident with the charge, "For imposing Taxes on us without our Consent." In particular, this charge refers to taxes enacted after the Sugar Act of 1764, as these would have been fresh in the minds of colonists at the time of the declaration's writing.

One of the most powerful charges was, "He has plundered our seas, ravaged our Coasts, burnt our towns, and destroyed the lives of our people." This referred to the British seizure of ships that violated certain laws made by the king in 1775, just one year before Jefferson wrote the Declaration of Independence. English troops by that time had also waged attacks on the seaport towns of Falmouth, which is now Portland, Maine; Bristol, Rhode Island; and Norfolk, Virginia. American sailors who were captured on ships that were said to violate these laws were required to join the British Navy. The British also recruited Native Americans, who resented the colonists' presence on their land, to fight against the colonists in frontier areas.

All these charges were directed only at the king, and not toward Parliament or the British people directly. In fact, the word "Parliament" is not mentioned at all in the Declaration of Independence. This was intentional, despite the fact that the colonies had for years argued back and forth with the British Parliament. Though it was Parliament that had enacted many of the laws that had angered the colonists, Jefferson was careful not to attack this institution of representative government. The Declaration of Independence was to be an attack on the tyranny of the king, and it was hoped that by avoiding a criticism of other British institutions many colonists who still felt loyalty to Britain could be brought over to the revolutionary cause.

The Closing Argument for Independence

The final paragraphs of the document consist of the actual declaration that the colonies "are, and of Right ought to be Free and Independent States . . ." It was Jefferson's closing argument for independence. The colonists felt that they had no other choice at this point but to break with England. As stated in the next to the last paragraph, they had tried appealing to the king and to their "British brethren," but to no avail. Yet, while a severing of political ties was desired, a softness of heart was expressed toward the British people, who were to be considered "Enemies in War, in Peace Friends."

The last sentence reflects the strength of the unity that now bonded the colonists: "And for the support of this Declaration, with a firm reliance on the protection of divine Providence, we mutually pledge to each other our Lives, our Fortunes and our sacred Honor."

Following the text are the now famous signatures of the drafting committee, the members of the Continental Congress, and other political notables. Most prominent is the signature of the president of the Continental Congress, John Hancock, who in an act of defiance wrote in huge letters so that a nearsighted English official would have no trouble identifying him.

The Legacy of the Declaration of Independence

The ideas in the Declaration of Independence have endured long after America won the American Revolution in 1783. In 1789, the French National Assembly adopted a document entitled the Declaration of the Rights of Man. Inspired by the Declaration of Independence, the Rights of Man helped to shape France during and after the French Revolution, which was taking place at this time.

During the War of 1812 the original, primary copy of the Declaration of Independence was quickly removed from Washington DC, just before British troops entered the area. Both the United States and the Declaration of Independence survived the attack.

During the American Civil War (1861–1865) the Declaration of Independence strengthened the battle cry for slavery's end in the states. Jefferson's passionate plea, stricken out of the declaration's rough draft, at last was transformed from words into action. Abraham Lincoln, who led the fight to end slavery and helped to save the union of the states, credited the 1776 document for much of his inspiration. While still a president-elect, Lincoln said:

> *I have often inquired of myself, which great principle or idea it was that kept this nation together. It was . . . something in that Declaration giving liberty, not alone to the people of this country, but hope to the world for all future time . . .*
>
> *It was that which gave promise that in due time the weights should be lifted from the shoulders*

The Declaration of Independence inspired Abraham Lincoln (1809–1865), sixteenth president of the United States, to fight for liberty when the country faced a civil war.

of all men, and that all should have an equal chance.

In the nineteenth and twentieth centuries, women seeking the right to vote often turned to the Declaration of Independence to support their fight, which was won in 1920 with the passage of the Nineteenth Amendment. In the 1960s and 1970s, the Declaration of Independence empowered activists during the civil rights and women's movements. In 2001, the document helped to comfort and strengthen the nation, which was grieving over the losses inflicted by terrorists on September 11.

In 1952, the US Constitution and the Declaration of Independence were moved to the National Archives building in Washington DC. These precious documents are stored under the tightest security. During the day, visitors from all over the nation and the world can view them through special impenetrable glass cases. At night, they are lowered underground into a massive steel and concrete vault.

In 1984, a memorial was erected in the National Mall's Constitution Gardens, in Washington DC. Visitors to this memorial can see signatures of each of the 56 delegates who signed the Declaration of Independence carved in stone.

As an object, the Declaration of Independence is extremely valuable. As a statement of the philosophy guiding and defining American life and as a reminder of the freedoms for which this nation has come to stand, the Declaration is priceless.

Appendix
The Declaration of Independence

Action of Second Continental Congress, July 4, 1776

The unanimous Declaration of the thirteen United States of America

WHEN in the Course of human Events, it becomes necessary for one People to dissolve the Political Bands which have connected them with another, and to assume among the Powers of the Earth, the separate and equal Station to which the Laws of Nature and of Nature's God entitle them, a decent Respect to the Opinions of Mankind requires that they should declare the causes which impel them to the Separation.

WE hold these Truths to be self-evident, that all Men are created equal, that they are endowed by their Creator with certain unalienable Rights, that among these are Life, Liberty and the Pursuit of Happiness— That to secure these Rights, Governments are instituted among Men, deriving their just Powers from the Consent of the Governed, that whenever any Form of Government becomes destructive of these Ends, it is the Right of the People to alter or to abolish it, and to institute new Government, laying its Foundation on such Principles, and organizing its Powers in such Form, as to them shall seem most likely to effect their Safety and Happiness. Prudence, indeed, will dictate that Governments long established should not be changed for light and transient Causes; and accordingly all Experience hath shewn, that Mankind are more disposed to suffer, while Evils are sufferable, than to right themselves by abolishing the Forms to which they are accustomed. But when a long Train of Abuses and Usurpations, pursuing invariably the same Object, evinces a Design to reduce them under absolute Despotism, it is their Right, it is their Duty, to throw off such Government, and to provide new Guards for their future Security. Such has been the patient Sufferance of these Colonies; and such is now the Necessity which constrains them to alter their former Systems of Government. The History of the present King of Great-Britain is a History of repeated Injuries and Usurpations, all having in direct Object the Establishment of an absolute Tyranny over these States. To prove this, let Facts be submitted to a candid World.

HE has refused his Assent to Laws, the most wholesome and necessary for the public Good.

HE has forbidden his Governors to pass Laws of immediate and pressing Importance, unless suspended in their Operation till his Assent should be obtained; and when so suspended, he has utterly neglected to attend to them.

HE has refused to pass other Laws for the Accommodation of large Districts of People, unless those People would relinquish the Right of Representation in the Legislature, a Right inestimable to them, and formidable to Tyrants only.

HE has called together Legislative Bodies at Places unusual, uncomfortable, and distant from the Depository of their public Records, for the sole Purpose of fatiguing them into Compliance with his Measures.

HE has dissolved Representative Houses repeatedly, for opposing with manly Firmness his Invasions on the Rights of the People.

HE has refused for a long Time, after such Dissolutions, to cause others to be elected; whereby the Legislative Powers, incapable of the Annihilation, have returned to the People at large for their exercise; the State remaining in the mean time exposed to all the Dangers of Invasion from without, and the Convulsions within.

HE has endeavoured to prevent the Population of these States; for that Purpose obstructing the Laws for

Naturalization of Foreigners; refusing to pass others to encourage their Migrations hither, and raising the Conditions of new Appropriations of Lands.

HE has obstructed the Administration of Justice, by refusing his Assent to Laws for establishing Judiciary Powers.

HE has made Judges dependent on his Will alone, for the Tenure of their Offices, and the Amount and Payment of their Salaries.

HE has erected a Multitude of new Offices, and sent hither Swarms of Officers to harrass our People, and eat out their Substance.

HE has kept among us, in Times of Peace, Standing Armies, without the consent of our Legislatures.

HE has affected to render the Military independent of and superior to the Civil Power.

HE has combined with others to subject us to a Jurisdiction foreign to our Constitution, and unacknowledged by our Laws; giving his Assent to their Acts of pretended Legislation:

FOR quartering large Bodies of Armed Troops among us:

FOR protecting them, by a mock Trial, from Punishment for any Murders which they should commit on the Inhabitants of these States:

FOR cutting off our Trade with all Parts of the World:

FOR imposing Taxes on us without our Consent:

FOR depriving us, in many Cases, of the Benefits of Trial by Jury:

FOR transporting us beyond Seas to be tried for pretended Offences:

FOR abolishing the free System of English Laws in a neighbouring Province, establishing therein an arbitrary Government, and enlarging its Boundaries, so as to render it at once an Example and fit Instrument for introducing the same absolute Rules into these Colonies:

FOR taking away our Charters, abolishing our most valuable Laws, and altering fundamentally the Forms of our Governments:

FOR suspending our own Legislatures, and declaring themselves invested with Power to legislate for us in all Cases whatsoever.

HE has abdicated Government here, by declaring us out of his Protection and waging War against us.

HE has plundered our Seas, ravaged our Coasts, burnt our Towns, and destroyed the Lives of our People.

HE is, at this Time, transporting large Armies of foreign Mercenaries to compleat the Works of Death, Desolation, and Tyranny, already begun with circumstances of Cruelty and Perfidy, scarcely paralleled in the most barbarous Ages, and totally unworthy the Head of a civilized Nation.

HE has constrained our fellow Citizens taken Captive on the high Seas to bear Arms against their Country, to become the Executioners of their Friends and Brethren, or to fall themselves by their Hands.

HE has excited domestic Insurrections amongst us, and has endeavoured to bring on the Inhabitants of our Frontiers, the merciless Indian Savages, whose known Rule of Warfare, is an undistinguished Destruction, of all Ages, Sexes and Conditions.

IN every stage of these Oppressions we have Petitioned for Redress in the most humble Terms: Our repeated Petitions have been answered only by repeated Injury. A Prince, whose Character is thus marked by every act which may define a Tyrant, is unfit to be the Ruler of a free People.

NOR have we been wanting in Attentions to our British Brethren. We have warned them from

Time to Time of Attempts by their Legislature to extend an unwarrantable Jurisdiction over us. We have reminded them of the Circumstances of our Emigration and Settlement here. We have appealed to their native Justice and Magnanimity, and we have conjured them by the Ties of our common Kindred to disavow these Usurpations, which, would inevitably interrupt our Connections and Correspondence. They too have been deaf to the Voice of Justice and of Consanguinity. We must, therefore, acquiesce in the Necessity, which denounces our Separation, and hold them, as we hold the rest of Mankind, Enemies in War, in Peace, Friends.

WE, therefore, the Representatives of the UNITED STATES OF AMERICA, in GENERAL CONGRESS, Assembled, appealing to the Supreme Judge of the World for the Rectitude of our Intentions, do, in the Name, and by Authority of the good People of these Colonies, solemnly Publish and Declare, That these United Colonies are, and of Right ought to be, FREE AND INDEPENDENT STATES; that they are absolved from all Allegiance to the British Crown, and that all political Connection between them and the State of Great-Britain, is and ought to be totally dissolved; and that as FREE AND INDEPENDENT STATES, they have full Power to levy War, conclude Peace, contract Alliances, establish Commerce, and to do all other Acts and Things which INDEPENDENT STATES may of right do. And for the support of this Declaration, with a firm Reliance on the Protection of divine Providence, we mutually pledge to each other our Lives, our Fortunes, and our sacred Honor.

New Hampshire:
Josiah Bartlett
William Whipple
 Matthew Thornton

Massachusetts:
John Hancock
Samual Adams
John Adams
Robert Treat Paine
Elbridge Gerry

Rhode Island:
Stephen Hopkins
William Ellery

Connecticut:
Roger Sherman
Samuel Huntington
William Williams
Oliver Wolcott

New York:
William Floyd
Philip Livingston
Francis Lewis
Lewis Morris

New Jersey:
Richard Stockton
John Witherspoon
Francis Hopkinson
John Hart, Abraham Clark

Pennsylvania:
Robert Morris
Benjamin Rush
Benjamin Franklin
John Morton
George Clymer
James Smith
George Taylor
James Wilson
George Ross

Delaware:
Caesar Rodney
George Read
Thomas McKean

Maryland:
Samuel Chase
William Paca
Thomas Stone
Charles Carroll of Carrollton

Virginia:
George Wythe
Richard Henry Lee
Thomas Jefferson
Benjamin Harrison
Thomas Nelson, Jr.
Francis Lightfoot Lee
Carter Braxton

North Carolina:
William Hooper
Joseph Hewes
John Penn

South Carolina:
Edward Rutledge
Thomas Heyward, Jr.,
Thomas Lynch, Jr.
Arthur Middleton

Georgia:
Button Gwinnett
Lyman Hall
George Walton

Glossary

Boston Massacre—An altercation between colonists and British soldiers in 1770 that resulted in the deaths of five young protesters.

Boston Tea Party—A protest against the Tea Act, which levied duties on non-British tea, where men boarded British ships and threw their cargo into Boston's harbor.

British Parliament—The supreme legislative body for Great Britain.

colonist—A person who settles in a new country.

Common Sense—A pamphlet authored by the radical patriot Thomas Paine that called for America's independence from Great Britain. Extremely popular in its day, the book fueled anti-British sentiment throughout the colonies.

Intolerable Acts—Laws passed by the British in 1774 that were meant to punish the colonists for the Boston Tea Party. They instead incited more anger among the colonists.

London Company—A group of British men and colonists who pledged money, organized, and established a settlement in America.

mercantilism—A system wherein colonies are required to send back raw materials to the mother country and are expected to purchase finished goods from businessmen there.

Molasses and Sugar Acts—Tax laws in the eighteenth century that put duties on sugar and molasses that colonists purchased from non-British sources.

Navigation Acts—Laws in the seventeenth century that limited colonial trade, giving greater control to England.

pilgrims—The English colonists who settled in Plymouth, Massachusetts, in 1620. They had left their mother country due to religious persecution.

Sons of Liberty—An organization of men, founded in the eighteenth century, which desired greater political independence in America.

Stamp Act—Passed in 1765, this law required that colonists buy stamps for printed items, such as newspapers and legal documents. The act was widely protested in America.

Townshend Acts—A series of laws passed in 1767 requiring the colonists to pay the British duties on glass, paper, dyes, and tea.

Virginia Declaration of Rights—A document, similar to the Declaration of Independence, written for the Virginia legislature. Thomas Jefferson borrowed many ideas from it, and it also later inspired the drafting of the Bill of Rights.

Further Reading

Driver, Stephanie Schwartz. *Understanding the Declaration of Independence.* New York: The Rosen Publishing Group, 2010.

Krensky, Stephen. *The Declaration of Independence.* New York: Marshall Cavendish Benchmark, 2012.

Marcovitz, Hal. *The Declaration of Independence.* Philadelphia: Mason Crest, 2014.

Meacham, Jon. *Thomas Jefferson.* New York: Random House, 2012.

Ransom, Candice F. *What Was the Continental Congress?* Minneapolis, Minn.: Lerner Publishing Group, 2011.

Swain, Gwenyth. *Documents of Freedom: A Look at the Declaration of Independence, the Bill of Rights, and the U.S. Constitution.* Minneapolis, Minn.: Lerner Publishing Group, 2012.

Web Sites

historians.org

The American Historical Association (AHA) is the largest professional organization in the United States devoted to the study and promotion of history and historical thinking.

independencemuseum.org

The American Independence Museum features stories of the brave men and women who overcame their uncertainties about freedom from Great Britain and established our country.

loc.gov

The Library of Congress is the nation's oldest federal cultural institution and serves as the research arm of Congress. The Library's mission is to support the Congress in fulfilling its constitutional duties and to further the progress of knowledge and creativity for the benefit of the American people.

monticello.org

Monticello, Thomas Jefferson's plantation near Charlottesville, Virginia, was the center of his world. To understand Jefferson, one must understand Monticello; it can be seen as his autobiographical statement.

nara.gov

The National Archives and Records Administration (NARA) is the nation's record keeper.

Chapter Notes

Chapter One. Life in the Colonies

1. Hugh Brogan, The *Pelican History of the United States of America* (London: Penguin Group, 1985), p. 33.
2. Brogan, p. 15.

Chapter Two. Growing Dissatisfaction

1. John L. Bullion, "Stamp Act," *World Book Online Americas Edition* (http://www.aolsvc.worldbook.aol.com/wbol/wbPage/na/ar/co/528680), May 7, 2002, p. 1.
2. Brogan, p. 72.
3. Ibid.

Chapter Three. Thomas Jefferson Drafts the Document

1. Carl L. Becker, *The Declaration of Independence: A Study in the History of Political Ideas* (New York: Vintage Books, 1958), p. 3.
2. Thomas Jefferson, "The Account of the Declaration: Jefferson's Story of the Declaration" (http://www.ushistory.org/declaration/account/acc3.htm), April 15, 2002, p. 1.

3. Page Smith, *Jefferson: A Revealing Biography* (New York: American Heritage Publishing Co., Inc., 1976) p. 93.

Chapter Four. No Original Ideas

1. Smith, p. 67.
2. Thomas Jefferson, *Writings* (New York: The Library of America, 1984), p. 105–106.
3. Becker, p. 24.
4. Jefferson, p. 1501.
5. John Locke, *Two Treatises of Civil Government* (London: J.M. Dent & Sons, Ltd., 1924), p. 119.
6. Locke, p. 120.
7. Jefferson, p. 1501.
8. George Mason, "The Virginia Declaration of Rights," *National Archives* (http://www.nara.gov/exhall/charters/billrights/virginia.html), April 15, 2002.
9. Thomas Paine, *Rights of Man and Common Sense* (New York: Alfred A. Knopf, Inc., 1994), p. 279.

Chapter Five. The Final Document

1. Herman J. Viola, *The National Archives of the United States* (New York: Henry N. Abrams, Inc., 1984), p. 56.

2. Thomas Jefferson, "The Account of the Declaration: Jefferson's Story of the Declaration, Rough Draft," (http://www.ushistory.org/declaration/account/d-draft.htm), April 15, 2002.
3. Ibid.
4. Ibid.
5. Ibid.
6. Thomas Jefferson, "The Account of the Declaration: Jefferson's Story of the Declaration, Congress' Draft" (http://www.ushistory.org/declaration/account/acc4.htm), April 15, 2002.
7. Frank Donovan, *Mr. Jefferson's Declaration: The Story Behind the Declaration of Independence* (New York: Dodd, Mead & Company, 1968), p. 94.

Chapter Six. Examining the Declaration of Independence

1. Thomas Fleming, *Liberty! The American Revolution* (New York: Viking, 1997), p. 176.

Index